LOW CALORIE

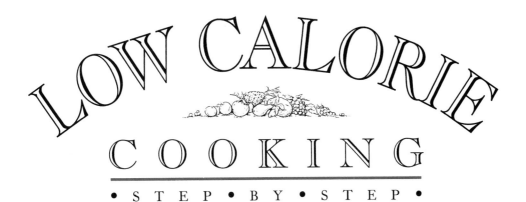

COOKING

· S T E P · BY · S T E P ·

® Landoll, Inc.
Ashland, Ohio 44805
Text and photographs
© 1995 Coombe Books Ltd.
Cover
© 1996 Landoll, Inc.

Introduction

Keeping a check on your weight is probably one of the best ways to improve your general health. By eating a nutritionally balanced, calorie-controlled diet you will be helping your body to become fitter and to function more efficiently. Being overweight increases the chances of high blood pressure, thrombosis and heart attack, it makes keeping fit more difficult and often leaves people with low self-esteem. This is not to suggest that we should all be "model-girl slim." Watching your weight simply means sustaining a healthy weight for your height and age.

Whether you are on a weight-reducing diet or are simply trying to sustain your present weight, it is important to balance the food you consume against the benefits obtained from it. A chocolate milkshake will provide you with a few important nutrients, but it will not provide you with sufficient amounts of fiber, vitamins or protein for one meal, nor will it educate you to rely upon a well balanced and regular diet.

Calorie counting is in fact an ideal way of checking, on a daily basis, that you are consuming the correct amount of calories to stay at your present weight. If the amount of calories being consumed does not exceed the amount of calories being expended, a constant body weight will be maintained. In this respect the significance of regular exercise cannot be ignored – the more active you are the easier weight control becomes. There are no fast solutions to maintaining a healthy weight, a nutritionally balanced, calorie-controlled diet in conjunction with regular exercise is the healthiest and most natural answer.

These recipes have been compiled to help you plan a regular pattern of eating which is both low in calories and high in enjoyment. All the recipes are calorie counted so all you have to do is set a realistic daily allowance and decide which of the easily prepared meals to include in your menu.

SERVES 4
44 kilocalories per serving

CARROT SOUP

Carrots make a most delicious soup which is both filling and extremely low in calories.

1lb carrots
1 medium-sized onion
1 medium-sized turnip
2 cloves garlic, minced
3 cups water or vegetable stock
¾ tsp dried thyme
¾ tsp ground nutmeg
Salt and ground white pepper to taste
Toasted sunflower seeds, slivered almonds and pistachio nuts, mixed together for garnish

1. Peel the carrots and cut them into thick slices.

2. Peel and roughly chop the onion and turnip.

3. Put the vegetables, garlic and water or stock, into a large saucepan and bring to the boil. Cover the pan, reduce the heat and simmer for 20 minutes.

4. Add all the seasonings and simmer for a further 5 minutes.

5. Remove the soup from the heat and allow to cool for 15 minutes.

6. Using a liquidizer or food processor, blend the soup until it is thick and smooth.

7. Reheat the soup as required, garnishing with the seeds and nuts before serving.

Step 2 Using a sharp knife, roughly chop the peeled onions and turnip.

Step 1 Cut the carrots into thick slices, approximately ½-inch thick.

Step 6 Purée the soup in a liquidizer or food processor, until it is thick and smooth.

Cook's Notes

Time
Preparation takes about 12 minutes, cooking takes 25-30 minutes.

Cook's Tip
Make the recipe in double quantities and freeze half for a future date.

Variation
Use ¼ tsp cayenne pepper in place of the nutmeg in this recipe.

SERVES 4
115 kilocalories per serving

MELON AND PROSCIUTTO

This typically Italian appetizer is wonderful served well chilled on warm summer days.

1 large ripe melon, either Galia or Honeydew
16 thin slices prosciutto ham
French flat leaf parsley to garnish

Step 1 Using a spoon, scoop out and discard the seeds and fibrous core of the melon.

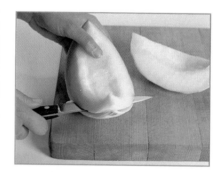

Step 2 Carefully remove the rind from the quartered melon, using a sharp knife.

Step 4 Roll a slice of prosciutto ham around each thin slice of melon.

1. Cut the melon in half lengthwise. Using a spoon, scoop out and discard all the seeds and fibers.

2. Cut the melon into quarters and carefully peel away the skin using a sharp knife.

3. Cut each quarter into 4 thin slices.

4. Wrap each slice of melon in a slice of the prosciutto ham, and arrange on a serving dish. Chill well and garnish with parsley before serving.

Cook's Notes

Time
Preparation takes 15 minutes.

Cook's Tip
Use this recipe, along with other items such as olives, stuffed eggs and sliced salami, as Italian antipasta for a buffet party.

Variation
Serve the slices of prosciutto ham in rolls, accompanied by quartered fresh figs in place of the melon.

SERVES 20

334 kilocalories per serving

SPICED BEEF

Spiced beef makes an attractive addition to a buffet or cold table and only a small serving is necessary for each guest. If you do not wish to cook a piece of meat this size, simply reduce the recipe by half.

6lb piece brisket, silverside, or topside of beef
3 bay leaves
1¼ tsps powdered mace
6 cloves
1¼ tsps black peppercorns
1¼ tsps allspice
2 large cloves garlic
2½ tbsps molasses
2½ tbsps brown sugar
1lb cooking salt
2¼ tsps saltpetre

1. Trim the excess fat from the piece of beef and make sure that it is well tied with string, so that it will keep its shape during the spicing.

2. Break the bay leaves into small pieces, and mix with the powdered mace.

3. Put the cloves, peppercorns and allspice into a mortar and crush them to a fine powder with a pestle.

4. Chop the garlic and add this to the crushed spices in the mortar, along with 1 tsp of the salt. Blend this to a paste, using the pestle.

5. Put the bay leaves, mace, ground spices, garlic, black treacle, brown sugar, cooking salt and the saltpetre in a very large bowl, and mix them together thoroughly.

6. Place the beef in a bowl, and rub all the surfaces thoroughly with the spicing mixture. Cover the bowl and set aside.

7. Repeat this process every day for 1 week, turning the meat and rubbing in the spices each day. Keep the meat in a cool place, or refrigerator, during this time.

8. To cook, cover the joint of beef with water in a very large saucepan. Bring the water to the boil, cover and simmer slowly for 6 hours. Allow the meat to cool in the cooking liquid.

9. Remove the cooled meat from the liquid, remove the string and place in a tight fitting dish or large loaf pan.

10. Put a plate on top of the piece of beef and weigh it down with balance scale weights or bags of sugar. Leave the beef to press in a cool place overnight.

11. To serve, slice the beef very thinly and serve cold on a bed of lettuce.

Step 6 Rub the surface of the beef evenly with some of the spicing mixture, making sure that all surface areas are well coated.

Step 8 Put the beef in a large pan and pour over enough water to cover.

Cook's Notes

Time
Preparation takes 1 week, cooking time takes approximately 6 hours.

Cook's Tip
Saltpetre can be purchased from any chemist.

Watchpoint
Make sure the beef in kept in a cool place whilst the spicing takes effect.

SERVES 4
24 kilocalories per serving

Orange, Grapefruit and Mint Salad

Fresh citrus fruits are complemented beautifully by the fragrant flavor of fresh mint. Serve chilled for an ideal low calorie appetizer.

2 grapefruits
3 oranges
Liquid sweetener to taste (optional)
8 sprigs of mint

1. Using a serrated knife, cut away the peel and the white pith from the grapefruit and the oranges.

2. Carefully cut inside the skin of each segment to remove each section of flesh.

3. Squeeze the membranes over a bowl to extract all the juice. Sweeten the juice with the liquid sweetener, if required.

4. Arrange the orange and the grapefruit segments in alternating colors on 4 individual serving dishes.

5. Using a sharp knife, chop 4 springs of the mint very finely. Stir the chopped mint into the fruit juice.

6. Carefully spoon the juice over the arranged fruit segments and chill thoroughly.

7. Garnish with a sprig of mint before serving.

Step 1 Using a serrated knife, cut away the peel from the grapefruits and the oranges, making sure that you remove all the white pith as you cut.

Step 2 Carefully cut inside the skin of each segment to remove each section of flesh, trying to keep each piece as intact as possible.

Cook's Notes

Time
Preparation takes about 20 minutes, plus chiling time.

Cook's Tip
This appetizer can be prepared up to a day in advance.

Preparation
Make sure all the white pith is removed from the fruit, as it produces a bitter flavor.

Variation
Use ruby grapefruits and blood oranges, when available, in place of the normal types of fruit for a colorful variation. Use borage leaves in place of the mint, and garnish with a few of the blue flowers.

SERVES 4

41 kilocalories per serving

INDIAN TOMATO SOUP

This highly fragrant and spicy tomato soup makes an interesting
low calorie appetizer.

½lb tomatoes
1 medium-sized onion
2½ tbsps vegetable oil
1 green chili, seeded and finely chopped
3 cloves garlic, minced
1¼ tbsps tomato paste
4½ cups water, or vegetable stock
4-6 green curry leaves, or ¾ tsp curry powder
Freshly ground sea salt to taste
Coriander leaves and green chilies for garnish

1. Cut a small cross in the skin of each tomato and plunge them into boiling water for 30-40 seconds.

2. Remove the tomatoes and carefully peel away the loosened skin with a sharp knife.

3. Remove the green core from the tomatoes and roughly chop the flesh.

4. Peel the onion and chop it into small pieces using a sharp knife.

5. Heat the oil in a large saucepan and gently sauté the onion, chopped chili and garlic for 3-4 minutes until it is soft, but not browned.

6. Stir in the chopped tomatoes and cook for 5 minutes, stirring often to prevent the vegetables from burning.

7. Blend the tomato paste with the water and pour this into the onions and tomatoes. Add the curry leaves or powder, season with the salt and simmer for 5-7 minutes.

8. Remove the soup from the heat and stir in the coriander leaves and the chili halves.

9. Pour the soup into 4-6 serving bowls and serve piping hot, discarding the chili garnish before eating.

Step 2 Remove the tomatoes from the boiling water and carefully peel away the loosened skin.

Step 3 Cut away and discard the hard green core from the tomatoes, and chop the flesh roughly with a sharp knife.

Cook's Notes

Time
Preparation takes about 15 minutes, cooking takes 17-18 minutes.

Watchpoint
Great care must be taken when preparing fresh chilies. Try not to get the juice into your eyes or mouth. If this should happen, rinse with lots of cold water.

Freezing
This soup freezes well, but should be frozen before adding the garnish.

SERVES 4

113 kilocalories per serving

"BURNT" PEPPER SALAD

Burning peppers under a hot broiler is a traditional way of preparing this sweet vegetable which enhances, rather than impairs, its subtle flavor.

3 large colored peppers, e.g. red, green and yellow
5 tbsps olive oil
1 clove garlic, finely chopped
8 basil leaves, roughly chopped
3 sprigs of fresh marjoram, roughly chopped
2½ tbsps fresh pickled capers
2½ tbsps white wine vinegar

1. Cut the peppers in half lengthwise. Remove and discard the core and seeds.

Step 2 Press the pepper halves down on a flat surface with the palm of your hands to flatten them completely.

2. Lay the peppers, cut side down, on a flat surface and flatten them out by pressing down with the palm of your hand.

3. Preheat the broiler to hot. Arrange the peppers on a broiler pan and brush with 1¼ tbsps of the olive oil.

4. Broil the peppers until the skins are well charred. Wrap them in a clean towel and leave for 15 minutes.

5. Unwrap the peppers and peel off the charred and

Step 4 Char the skin of the peppers under a hot broiler, turning them around, if necessary, to burn evenly.

Step 5 Wrap the charred peppers in a cloth to retain the moisture and lift the charred skins away from the pepper flesh.

loosened skin.

6. Cut the peppers into thick strips and arrange them onto a serving dish.

7. Scatter over the chopped garlic, basil leaves, marjoram and capers.

8. Mix together the remaining olive oil and the vinegar, and pour over the peppers. Refrigerate for at least 1 hour before serving.

Cook's Notes

Time
Preparation takes about 30 minutes, plus 1 hour chiling time.

Variation
For a special occasion use nasturtium flower buds instead of the capers.

Preparation
The skins of the peppers must be very well charred on the outside before wrapping them in the towel, otherwise their skin will not peel away properly.

Cook's Tip
If you do not wish to broil the peppers, pierce the whole pepper with a fork and hold them over a gas flame to char the skin.

SERVES 2

252 kilocalories per serving

FRESH TOMATO OMELET

Omelets can make substantial low calorie lunches or light meals and can be varied by using different fillings. This recipe uses lots of tasty fresh tomatoes, which can be eaten in abundance on a calorie controlled diet.

1lb fresh tomatoes
Salt and freshly ground black pepper
4 eggs
5 tbsps water
¾ tsp fresh chopped basil
2½ tbsps olive or vegetable oil
¾ tsp fresh chopped oregano or basil to garnish

1. Cut a small cross into the skins of each tomato and plunge them into boiling water. Leave for 30 seconds, then remove them with a draining spoon.

2. Using a sharp knife carefully peel away the tomato skins and discard them.

3. Cut the tomatoes in half and remove and discard the seeds, juice and any tough core.

4. Cut the tomato flesh into thin strips.

5. Break the eggs into a bowl and beat in the water and chopped herbs. Season with salt and pepper and continue beating until the egg mixture is frothy.

6. Heat the oil in a large frying pan or skillet, then pour in the egg mixture.

7. Using a spatula, stir the egg mixture around the skillet for about 2-3 minutes, or until the eggs are beginning to set.

8. Spread the tomato strips over the partially cooked eggs, and continue cooking without stirring until the eggs have completely set and the tomatoes are just warmed through.

9. Sprinkle with the additional chopped basil before serving.

Step 2 Carefully peel away and discard the tomato skins from the blanched fruit, using a sharp knife.

Step 3 Remove the seeds and juice from the halved tomatoes with a teaspoon.

Step 5 Beat the eggs, water and herbs together thoroughly, until they are frothy.

Cook's Notes

Time
Preparation takes about 25 minutes, cooking takes about 5 minutes.

Variation
Add 1 clove of minced garlic to the egg mixture, if desired.

Serving Idea
Cut the omelet into wedges and serve straight from the frying pan.

SERVES 4
83 kilocalories per serving
VEGETABLE KEBABS

A colorful and flavorsome way to serve delicious fresh vegetables as part of a low calorie diet.

1 large eggplant
Salt
1 large green pepper
4 zucchini
12-14 cherry tomatoes, red or yellow
12-14 pickling onions
12-14 button mushrooms
5 tbsps olive oil
2½ tbsps lemon juice
¾ tsp salt
¾ tsp freshly ground black pepper

1. Cut the eggplant in half and dice it into 1-inch pieces.

2. Put the eggplant pieces into a large bowl, and sprinkle liberally with salt. Stir well and allow to stand for 30 minutes to degorge.

3. Rinse the eggplant pieces thoroughly in a colander under cold water, to remove all traces of salt.

4. Cut the green pepper in half. Remove and discard the core and seeds. Cut the pepper flesh into 1-inch pieces with a sharp knife.

5. Slice the zucchini diagonally into pieces approximately 1-inch thick.

6. Remove the tough cores form the cherry tomatoes and peel the onions. Rinse the mushrooms under cold water to remove any bits of soil, but do not peel.

7. Put all the prepared vegetables into a large bowl and pour in the remaining ingredients. Mix well to coat evenly, cover with plastic wrap and allow to stand for about 30 minutes, stirring the vegetables once or twice to ensure they remain evenly coated.

8. Thread the vegetables alternately onto skewers and arrange them on a broiler pan.

9. Brush the kebabs with the marinade and broil for 3-4 minutes, turning frequently and basting with the marinade until they are evenly browned. Serve piping hot.

Step 5 Cut the zucchini diagonally into 1-inch pieces.

Step 8 Thread the prepared and marinated vegetables alternately onto kebab skewers, keeping an even number of vegetable pieces on each skewer.

Cook's Notes

Time
Preparation takes about 30 minutes. Cooking takes about 10 minutes, plus time for the vegetables to marinate.

Preparation
It is important to degorge the eggplant before cooking, as this removes the bitterness from the flavor and some of the moisture as well.

Variation
Use any combination of your favorite vegetables in this recipe.

SERVES 6
213 kilocalories per serving

DOLMAS

Delicious individual parcels of rice, herbs, nuts and fruit, make a very different low calorie lunch or supper dish.

12 large cabbage leaves, washed
1 cup long grain rice
8 green onions
1¼ tbsps fresh chopped basil
1¼ tbsps fresh chopped mint
1¼ tbsps fresh chopped parsley
½ cup pine nuts
⅓ cup currants
Salt and freshly ground black pepper
5 tbsps olive oil
Juice 1 lemon
⅔ cup unset natural yogurt
¼lb cucumber

1. Using a sharp knife trim away any tough stems from the cabbage leaves.

2. Put the leaves into boiling water for about 30 seconds. Remove them using a slotted spoon and drain thoroughly before laying them out flat on a work surface.

3. Put the rice into a saucepan along with enough boiling water to just cover. Cook for 15-20 minutes, or until the rice is soft and the liquid almost completely absorbed. Rinse the rice in cold water to remove any starchiness.

4. Cut the green onions into thin diagonal slices. Put the rice and the chopped onions into a large bowl along with all the remaining ingredients, except 2½ tbsps olive oil, the yogurt and cucumber. Mix the rice mixture thoroughly to blend evenly.

5. Place about 2 tbsps of the rice filling onto each blanched cabbage leaf, pressing it gently into a sausage shape.

Step 5 Pile tablespoons of the filling onto the blanched leaves, pressing it gently into sausage shapes in the center of the leaves.

6. Fold the sides of the leaves over to partially cover the stuffing, and then roll up, jelly roll fashion, to completely envelop the filling.

7. Place the rolls seam side down in a large baking dish. Brush with the remaining olive oil. Pour hot water around the cabbage leaves until it comes about halfway up their sides.

8. Cover the baking dish with aluminum foil, pressing it gently onto the surface of the leaves to keep them in place. Bake in a preheated oven 375°F for 30-40 minutes.

9. Peel the cucumber and cut it lengthwise into quarters. Remove the pips and discard. Chop the cucumber flesh and half of the peel into very small pieces.

10. Mix the chopped cucumber into the yogurt and chill until required.

11. Drain the dolmas from the cooking liquid and arrange on a serving plate with a little of the cucumber sauce spooned over.

Cook's Notes

Time
Preparation takes about 30 minutes, cooking takes 40 minutes.

Serving Idea
Serve the dolmas either hot or cold.

Preparation
Dolmas can be prepared a day in advance and allowed to stand in their liquid in the refrigerator. They can be reheated just before serving if required.

Variation
Use any other ingredients you particularly like in the filling along with the rice. Use vine leaves instead of cabbage leaves in this recipe.

SERVES 6
156 kilocalories per serving

EGGPLANT BAKE

Eggplants are wonderfully filling vegetables with very few calories – the ideal ingredient in a calorie controlled diet.

2 large or 3 medium-sized eggplants
2½ tsps salt
⅔ cup malt vinegar
2½ tbsps vegetable oil
2 large onions, peeled and sliced into rings
2 green chilies, seeded and finely chopped
2 cups peeled plum tomatoes, chopped
¾ tsp chili powder
1¼ tsps minced garlic
¾ tsp ground turmeric
8 tomatoes, sliced
1⅓ cups natural unset yogurt
1¼ tsps freshly ground black pepper
1 cup Cheddar cheese, finely grated

1. Cut the eggplants into ¼-inch thick slices. Arrange the slices in a shallow dish and sprinkle with 1½ tsps of the salt. Pour over the malt vinegar, cover the dish and marinate for 30 minutes.

2. Drain the eggplant well, discarding the marinade liquid.

3. Heat the vegetable oil in a frying pan and gently fry the onion rings until they are golden brown.

4. Add the chilies, the remaining salt, chopped tomatoes, chili powder, garlic and turmeric. Mix well and simmer for 5-7 minutes until thick and well blended.

5. Remove the sauce from the heat and cool slightly. Blend to a smooth purée using a liquidizer or food processor.

6. Arrange half of the eggplant slices in the base of a lightly greased shallow ovenproof dish.

7. Spoon half of the tomato sauce over the eggplant slices. Cover the tomato sauce with the remaining eggplant, and then top this with the remaining tomato sauce and sliced tomatoes.

8. Mix together the yogurt, the freshly ground black pepper and the Cheddar cheese. Pour this mixture over the tomato slices.

9. Preheat an oven to 375°F, and cook the eggplant bake for 20-30 minutes, or until the cheese topping bubbles and turns golden brown. Serve hot straight from the oven.

Step 4 Fry the chilies, tomatoes and seasoning with the golden onion rings until they are softened and juice flows.

Step 7 Spoon half the tomato sauce over the eggplant slices in the gratin dish.

Cook's Notes

Time
Preparation takes about 30 minutes, cooking takes 40 minutes.

Preparation
Make sure that the eggplants are well drained when they are removed from the marinade. Press them into a colander using the back of your hand, to remove all excess vinegar. Do not rinse, as the vinegar gives a tangy flavor to the dish.

Cook's Tip
Use a low calorie cheese in place of the Cheddar cheese to reduce the calorie content further.

SERVES 4
54 kilocalories per serving

OKRA CASSEROLE

Okra has an interesting texture and a mild flavor which combines well with tomatoes to make this delicious Mediterranean-style casserole.

2½ tbsps olive oil
1 small onion
½lb fresh okra
6 ripe tomatoes
Juice of ½ lemon
Salt and freshly ground black pepper
2½ tbsps fresh chopped parsley

---

1. Peel the onions and cut them in half lengthwise. Use a sharp knife to cut them across in slices.

2. Heat the oil in a large saucepan and cook the onion until it is soft and transparent, but not browned.

3. Remove just the stems from the okra, but leave on the pointed tail. Take care not to cut off the very top of the okra.

4. Add the okra to the onions and cook gently for 10 minutes, stirring occasionally.

5. Cut a small cross into the skins of the tomatoes, and plunge them into boiling water for 30 seconds.

6. Drain the tomatoes and carefully peel away and discard the loosened skins. Chop the peeled fruit roughly.

7. Add the tomatoes, lemon juice, seasoning and parsley to the okra, and continue to cook for about 5 more minutes, or until the tomatoes are just heated through.

8. Spoon into a serving dish and serve hot or cold.

Step 3 Trim just the stems from the top of the okra, but take care not to remove the whole top, or the pointed tails.

Step 1 Place the halved peeled onions cut side downwards, and use a sharp knife to cut across into thin slices.

Step 6 Carefully peel the skins away from the blanched tomatoes, using a sharp knife.

Cook's Notes

Time
Preparation takes 15 minutes, cooking takes approximately 15 minutes.

Variation
Green beans can be used in place of the okra.

Cook's Tip
If you cannot get fresh okra, use canned okra in its place, but drain and rinse this before use and cut the cooking time in half.

Watchpoint
If too much liquid is left at the end of cooking, remove the vegetables with a slotted spoon and boil the liquid quickly to reduce the sauce.

SERVES 6

234 kilocalories per serving

PASTA WITH FRESH TOMATO AND BASIL SAUCE

Pasta is a good item to include on a low calorie diet, as it is very filling and can be served with any variety of low calorie sauces.

1 small onion, finely chopped
1lb fresh tomatoes
2½ tbsps tomato paste
1 orange
2 cloves garlic, minced
Salt and freshly ground black pepper
⅔ cup red wine
⅔ cup chicken stock
2½ tbsps coarsely chopped basil
1¾ cups whole-wheat pasta

1. Peel and finely chop the onion.

2. Cut a small cross in the skins of the tomatoes and plunge them into boiling water for 30 seconds. Remove the blanched tomatoes from the water and carefully peel away the loosened skin.

3. Cut the tomatoes into quarters, and remove and discard the pips. Chop the tomato flesh roughly, and put this, the onion and the tomato paste into a large saucepan.

4. Heat the onion and tomatoes over a gentle heat, stirring continuously until the tomatoes soften and begin to lose their juice.

5. Finely grate the rind from the orange. Cut the orange in half and squeeze out the juice.

6. Put the orange, rind and juice into a large saucepan along with all the remaining ingredients, and bring to the boil.

Step 1 To chop an onion finely, pierce the peeled onion with a fork and use this to hold the vegetable steady whilst you chop with a sharp knife.

Step 3 Cut the tomatoes into quarters and remove and discard the seeds.

7. Continue to boil until the sauce has reduced and thickened and the vegetables are soft.

8. Whilst the sauce is cooking, put the pasta into another saucepan with enough boiling water to cover. Season with a little salt and cook for 10-15 minutes, or until the pasta is soft.

9. Drain the pasta in a colander, and stir it into the hot sauce. Serve at once with a salad.

Cook's Notes

Time
Preparation takes 15-20 minutes, cooking takes 10-15 minutes.

Variation
Add ½ cup thinly sliced mushrooms to the sauce, if liked.

Freezing
This sauce will freeze very well for up to 3 months.

SERVES 6
153 kilocalories per serving

VEGETABLE AND OLIVE CASSEROLE

The addition of vinegar and capers gives this refreshing vegetable dish a sharp twist to its flavor.

1 eggplant
Salt
⅔ cup olive, or vegetable oil
1 onion, peeled and thinly sliced
2 red peppers, seeded and chopped
2 sticks of celery, sliced thickly
1lb canned plum tomatoes
2½ tbsps red wine vinegar
1¼ tbsps sugar
1 clove garlic, minced
12 black olives, pitted
1¼ tbsps capers
Salt and freshly ground black pepper

1. Cut the eggplant in half lengthwise and score the cut surface deeply, in a lattice fashion, with the point of a sharp knife.

2. Sprinkle the cut surface of the eggplant liberally with salt, and leave to stand for 30 minutes.

3. Rinse the eggplants thoroughly under running water, then pat dry and cut it into 1-inch cubes.

4. Heat the oil in a large sauté pan and add the onion, peppers and celery. Cook gently for about 5 minutes, stirring occasionally until the vegetables have softened but not browned.

5. Add the eggplant to the pan and mix well to coat thoroughly with the oil. Continue cooking gently for 5 minutes.

6. Chop the plum tomatoes and then press them through a nylon sieve, using the back of a wooden spoon to press out all the juice and pulp, leaving the seeds and pith in the sieve.

7. Add the sieved tomatoes to the vegetables in the sauté pan, along with the remaining ingredients, except for the olives and capers. Cover and simmer for 5 minutes.

8. Cut the olives into quarters and add these to the simmering vegetables, along with the capers.

9. Continue cooking gently, uncovered, for a further 15 minutes, or until most of the liquid has evaporated and the sauce has thickened and reduced.

Step 1 Score the cut surface of the eggplants in a lattice pattern, using the point of a sharp knife.

Step 9 Simmer the casserole, uncovered, over a low heat until the juice has thickened and reduced.

Cook's Notes

Time
Preparation takes 30 minutes, plus 30 minutes for the eggplants to degorge. Cooking takes approximately 25 minutes.

Preparation
Scoring and salting the eggplant will remove any bitter taste and toughness from the vegetable. Be very sure, however, to rinse all the salt off the eggplant before cooking, or this will affect the flavor of the dish.

Cook's Tip
This recipe may be prepared 2-3 days in advance and kept covered in a refrigerator.

Serving Idea
This recipe is delicious served cold as a salad, or hot with rice and pitta bread.

SERVES 6

21 kilocalories per serving

SALADE PAYSANNE

This homely salad can be made with any selection of fresh vegetables you have to hand. So whether its winter or summer, there's no excuse for not serving a delicious fresh salad.

4 green onions
½ cucumber
3 carrots
6 large tomatoes
10 button mushrooms
3 stems celery
1 green pepper, seeded and chopped
15-20 tiny cauliflower flowerets
15-20 radishes, quartered
1 tbsp chopped watercress, or mustard and cress
2 sprigs fresh green coriander leaf, or chopped parsley
¾ tsp salt
¾ tsp freshly ground black pepper
2½ tbsps cider vinegar
1¼ tbsps lemon juice
5 tbsps olive or vegetable oil
Pinch mustard powder
Liquid sweetener to taste
8 lettuce leaves for garnish

Step 3 Cut the carrot into thin pieces, slicing diagonally with a sharp knife.

Step 9 Whisk all the dressing ingredients together using a fork or eggbeater whisk, until the mixture becomes thick and cloudy.

1. Trim the green onions and slice them diagonally into thin slices.

2. Peel the cucumber and quarter it lengthwise. Use a sharp knife to remove the soft, seedy center, discard this, and dice the remaining flesh.

3. Peel and carrots and slice them thinly, cutting the carrots diagonally with a sharp knife.

4. Cut a small cross into the skins of each tomato, and plunge into boiling water for 30 seconds. Remove the tomatoes and carefully peel away the blanched skin from the fruit. Quarter the peeled tomatoes and cut away the tough green stalk.

5. Thinly slice the mushrooms and sticks of celery.

6. Cut the pepper in half lengthwise and remove all the seeds and the white pith. Discard this, and chop the flesh.

7. Break the cauliflower flowerets into small pieces, and quarter the radishes.

8. Roughly chop the watercress, or mustard and cress, along with the coriander leaves or parsley.

9. For the dressing mix together all the remaining ingredients, except for the lettuce leaves. Whisk thoroughly using a fork, or eggbeater, until the mixture becomes thick and cloudy.

10. Arrange the lettuce leaves on a serving dish, and pile the prepared vegetables on top.

11. Just before serving, spoon a little of the dressing over the salad and serve the remainder separately in a small jug.

Cook's Notes

Time
Preparation takes about 20 minutes.

Variation
Use any combination of your own favorite vegetables in this recipe.

Serving Idea
Serve with cheese or chicken for a light lunch.

SERVES 4
87 kilocalories per serving

BLACK OLIVE AND CAULIFLOWER SALAD

The exciting flavors of the Mediterranean combine in this recipe to produce a refreshingly different salad.

⅔ cup black olives
1 large cauliflower
1 large Spanish onion
5 tbsps olive oil
⅔ cup water
Juice ½ lemon
3½ tbsps tomato paste
Salt and freshly ground black pepper
2½ tbsps fresh chopped parsley

Step 1 To loosen the stones before pitting, roll the olives firmly on a flat surface using the palm of your hand.

1. Roll the olives firmly on a flat surface with the palm of your hands to loosen the stones. Remove the stones using a cherry pitter or the tip of a potato peeler. Chop the olives roughly and set aside.

2. Trim the leaves from the cauliflower and break it into small flowerets.

3. Peel the onion and slice it into rings.

4. Heat the oil in a large sauté pan and gently cook the cauliflower for 2 minutes. Remove the cauliflower to a plate, and cook the onion in the same pan, in the same way.

5. Return the cauliflower to the pan and add the water and the lemon juice. Bring to the boil, reduce the heat and simmer until tender, adding a little more water should the mixture begin to boil dry.

6. Using a slotted spoon, remove the cauliflower from the sauté pan, reserving the juices.

Step 3 Slice the onion into rings by piercing the peeled vegetable with a fork to hold it steady whilst you slice.

7. Add the tomato paste to the liquid and boil rapidly to reduce.

8. Stir the olives into the pan and heat through.

9. Arrange the cauliflower flowerets on a serving dish, and spoon the olive sauce over the top. Chill well.

10. Sprinkle with the chopped parsley just before serving.

Cook's Notes

Time
Preparation takes about 20 minutes, cooking takes approximately 20 minutes, plus chiling time.

Cook's Tip
Add a bay leaf to the cauliflower during the cooking to reduce the strong smell.

Variation
Use green olives instead of black.

SERVES 4
99 kilocalories per serving

STIR-FRIED SALAD

Stir fries are served hot, but the ingredients are cooked so quickly that they retain all of their crunchiness.

1 onion
2 large leeks
5 tbsps olive oil
2 cloves garlic, minced
½lb snow peas, topped and tailed
¼lb bean sprouts, or lentil sprouts
Salt and freshly ground black pepper
1 tbsp fresh chopped coriander leaf

1. Peel the onion and cut it into thin rings.

Step 1 Pierce the onion with a fork to hold it steady whilst you slice it into thin rings.

2. Trim the leeks and cut down the length of one side. Open the leek out and wash it thoroughly under running water.

3. Cut the leek into three pieces, then thinly slice each piece lengthwise into thin strips.

4. Heat the oil in a large wok or frying pan, and add the onions and garlic. Cook for 2 minutes, stirring all the time until the onions have softened but not browned.

5. Add the snow peas and sliced leeks to the wok and continue stir-frying for 4 minutes.

6. Add the remaining ingredients and cook briskly for a further 2 minutes. Serve piping hot.

Step 2 Rinse the split leek under running water, separating the leaves to wash out any grit or dirt.

Step 3 Cut the pieces of leek lengthwise into thin strips.

Cook's Notes

Time
Preparation takes 15 minutes, cooking takes approximately 10 minutes.

Cook's Tip
Sprout your own beans or lentils by putting them into a glass jar, rinse thoroughly and pour in fresh water each day, cover with muslin, and stand the jar on a sunny windowsill. After 3-4 days, the beans or lentils will have sprouted.

Serving Idea
Serve this dish with rice, and sprinkle it liberally with soy sauce.

SERVES 6
84 kilocalories per serving

RATATOUILLE

This delicious vegetable casserole from the south of France has become a great favorite the world over.

---

2 eggplants
Salt
4 zucchini
5 tbsps olive oil
2 Spanish onions
2 green or red peppers
2½ tsps chopped fresh basil
1 large clove garlic, minced
2 x 1lb 12 oz cans of peeled plum tomatoes
Salt and freshly ground black pepper
⅔ cup dry white wine

1. Cut the eggplants in half lengthwise and score each cut surface diagonally, using the point of a sharp knife.

2. Sprinkle the eggplants liberally with salt and allow to stand for 30 minutes to degorge. After this time, rinse them thoroughly and pat them dry.

3. Roughly chop the eggplants and slice the zucchini thickly. Set them to one side.

4. Peel the onions and half them. Cut them into thin slices with a sharp knife.

5. Cut the peppers in half lengthwise and remove and discard the seeds and white pith. Chop the flesh roughly.

6. Heat the oil in a large saucepan, and fry the onion slices for 5 minutes until they are soft and just beginning to brown.

7. Stir in the peppers and zucchini, and cook gently for 5 minutes until they begin to soften. Remove all the vegetables from the pan and set them aside.

8. Put the chopped eggplants into the saucepan with the

Step 5 Remove and discard the seeds and white pith from the halved peppers.

Step 8 Gently fry the chopped eggplant in the vegetable juices and oil, until they begin to brown.

vegetable juices. Cook gently until it begins to brown, then add all the other ingredients to the pan.

9. Add the cans of tomatoes, the garlic and the basil to the saucepan along with the sautéed vegetables, mixing well to blend in evenly. Bring to the boil, then reduce the heat and simmer for 15 minutes, or until the liquid in the pan has been reduced and is thick.

10. Add the wine to the pan and continue cooking for a further 15 minutes, before serving straight away, or chiling and serving cold.

Cook's Notes

Time
Preparation takes 20 minutes, plus 30 minutes standing time. Cooking takes approximately 35 minutes.

Preparation
Make sure that the degorged eggplant is rinsed thoroughly to remove any saltiness, otherwise this will spoil the flavor of the finished dish.

Cook's Tip
If the liquid in the pan is still thin and excessive after the full cooking time, remove the vegetables and boil the juices rapidly until they have reduced and thickened.

SERVES 4
239 kilocalories per serving

LIME ROASTED CHICKEN

*This simply made, but unusual, main course is very low in calories and high
in tangy flavor.*

4 chicken breast portions, each weighing about 8oz
Salt and freshly ground black pepper
4 limes
2½ tsps white wine vinegar
6 tbsps olive oil
2½ tsps fresh chopped basil

1. Rub the chicken portions all over with salt and black pepper. Place in a shallow ovenproof dish, and set aside.

2. Carefully pare away thin strips of the rind only from 2 of the limes, using a lemon parrer. Cut these 2 limes in half and squeeze the juice.

3. Add the lime juice to the vinegar and 4 tbsps of the olive oil in a small dish, along with the strips of rind, and mix well.

4. Pour the oil and lime juice mixture over the chicken por-

tions in the dish. Cover and refrigerate for about 4 hours or overnight.

5. Remove the covering from the dish in which the chicken is marinating, and baste the chicken well with the marinade mixture. Place into a preheated oven 375°F and cook for 30-35 minutes, or until the chicken is well roasted and tender.

6. In the meantime, peel away the rind and white pith from the remaining 2 limes. Cut the limes into thin slices using a sharp knife.

7. Heat the remaining oil in a small frying pan and add the lime slices and basil. Cook quickly for 1 minute, or until the fragrance rises up from the basil and the limes just begin to soften.

8. Serve the chicken portions on a serving platter, garnished with the fried lime slices and a little extra fresh basil, if desired.

Step 5 After marinating for 4 hours, the chicken portions will look slightly cooked and the meat will have turned a pale opaque color.

Step 7 Fry the lime slices very quickly in the hot oil until they just begin to soften.

Cook's Notes

Time
Preparation takes 25 minutes, plus 4 hours marinating time. Cooking takes 40 minutes.

Preparation
The chicken can be prepared in advance and marinated overnight.

Variation
Use lemons instead of limes, and thyme instead of basil.

Watchpoint
Puncture the chicken with a skewer at its thickest point and when the resulting juices run clear, it is ready.

SERVES 4
230 kilocalories per serving

PAPRIKA SCHNITZEL

Thin slices of pork tenderloin are served with a rich tasting paprika sauce for a delicious low calorie meal.

8 thin slices pork tenderloin cut along the fillet
Salt and freshly ground black pepper
1 clove garlic, minced
3¾ tbsps vegetable oil
1 medium-sized onion
1 red pepper
1 green pepper
1¼ tbsps paprika
⅔ cup beef stock
½ cup red wine
3¾ tbsps tomato paste
⅔ cup natural low fat yogurt

Step 1 Flatten the pork slices out with a rolling pin until they are ¼-inch thick.

1. Trim the slices of pork to remove any fat, and flatten them out with a rolling pin until they are ¼-inch thick.

2. Rub both sides of the pork slices with salt, pepper, and garlic, then allow to stand in a refrigerator for 30 minutes.

3. Heat the oil in a large frying pan, and cook the pork slices in several batches if necessary, until they are well browned and cooked right through. This will take approximately 4 minutes on each side.

4. Remove the pork from the pan, set aside, and keep warm.

5. Peel the onion and thinly slice it into rings, steadying it with a fork as you cut. Cut the peppers in half and remove and discard the seeds and white pith. Slice the peppers lengthwise into thin strips.

6. Add the onion rings and the sliced peppers to the oil and meat juices in the frying pan, and cook quickly for about 3-4 minutes until they are soft but not browned.

7. Add the paprika, stock, wine and tomato paste to the frying pan with the vegetables, and bring the mixture to the boil.

8. Reduce the heat and simmer until the liquid has evapo-

Step 6 Fry the onions and peppers together for 3-4 minutes until they have softened but not browned.

rated and the sauce has thickened. Season with salt and pepper to taste.

9. Arrange the pork slices on a serving dish, and pour the paprika sauce over the top of them.

10. Beat the yogurt in a bowl until it is smooth.

11. Carefully drizzle the yogurt over the paprika sauce to make an attractive pattern. Swirl it gently into the sauce to blend, but take care not to incorporate it completely. Serve hot.

Cook's Notes

Time
Preparation takes 30 minutes, cooking takes approximately 20 minutes.

Freezing
This dish freezes well.

Preparation
This dish may be made in advance, covered with foil, then reheated in a moderate oven when required.

Cook's Tip
If the yogurt is too thick to drizzle properly, whisk in a little water or skim milk to thin it to the required consistency.

SERVES 4
300 kilocalories per serving

CHICKEN ESCALOPES

Chicken is an excellent meat to eat when on a low calorie diet, as it is extremely low in fat. There are a multitude of different methods of cooking chicken, and this one although one of the simplest, is also one of the most delicious.

---

4 chicken breasts, boned and skinned
1 egg white
10 tbsps whole-wheat breadcrumbs
1¼ tbsps chopped fresh sage
Salt and freshly ground black pepper
2½ tbsps walnut oil
½ cup low calorie mayonnaise
⅔ cup natural unset yogurt
1¼ tsps grated fresh horseradish
2½ tbsps chopped walnuts
Lemon slices and chopped walnuts to garnish

---

1. Pat the chicken breasts dry with paper towels.

2. Whisk the egg whites with a fork until they just begin to froth, but are still liquid.

3. Carefully brush all surfaces of the chicken breasts with the beaten egg white.

4. Put the breadcrumbs onto a shallow plate and mix in the chopped sage. Season with a little salt and freshly ground black pepper.

5. Place the chicken breasts, one at a time, onto the plate of breadcrumbs and sage, and carefully press this mixture onto the surfaces of the chicken.

6. Put the oil into a large shallow pan, and gently fry the prepared chicken breasts on each side for 5 minutes until they are lightly golden and tender. Set them aside, and keep warm.

7. Mix all the remaining ingredients except for the garnish, in a small bowl, whisking well to blend the yogurt and mayonnaise evenly.

8. Place the cooked chicken breasts on a serving dish, and spoon a little of the sauce over. Serve garnished with the lemon slices and additional chopped nuts.

Step 2 Whisk the egg white with a fork until it becomes frothy, but still liquid.

Step 5 Press the breadcrumb and sage mixture onto all surfaces of the chicken breasts, making sure that they are covered evenly.

Cook's Notes

Time
Preparation takes about 20 minutes, cooking takes 10-15 minutes.

Variation
Use almonds instead of walnuts in this recipe, and limes instead of lemons. Oranges and hazelnuts make another delicious variation.

Serving Idea
Serve with lightly cooked green beans and new potatoes, or rice.

SERVES 4
198 kilocalories per serving

CHICKEN WITH BLACKCURRANT SAUCE

The sharp tang of blackcurrants makes an ideal partner for lightly cooked chicken.

4 chicken breasts, boned and skinned
4 tbsps sesame oil
1⅓ cups fresh blackcurrants
Juice of 1 orange
⅔ cup red wine
Artificial sweetener to taste
Orange slices and fresh blackcurrants to garnish

1. Season the chicken breasts with a little salt. Heat the oil in a shallow frying pan.

Step 2 Gently fry the chicken breasts in the hot oil until they are golden brown on all sides.

2. Gently fry the chicken breasts for 4-5 minutes on each side, until they are golden brown and tender.

3. Top and tail the blackcurrants and put them into a small pan, along with the orange juice and red wine. Bring to the boil, then cover and simmer gently until the blackcurrants are soft.

4. Using a liquidizer or food processor, blend the blackcurrants and the cooking juice for 30 seconds.

Step 5 Press the blackcurrant purée through a metal sieve with a wooden spoon, to remove all the pips and skins.

Step 6 Simmer the sieved fruit purée until it has thickened and the liquid has reduced.

5. Rub the blended purée through a nylon sieve with the back of a spoon, pressing the fruit through to reserve all the juice and pulp but leaving the pips in the sieve.

6. Put the sieved purée into a small saucepan and heat gently, stirring constantly until the liquid has reduced and the sauce is thick and smooth.

7. Arrange the chicken breasts on a serving dish, and spoon the blackcurrant sauce over. Garnish with orange slices and fresh blackcurrants.

Cook's Notes

Time
Preparation takes 15 minutes, cooking takes approximately 15 minutes.

Preparation
To test if the chicken breasts are cooked, insert a skewer into the thickest part, then press gently, if the juices run clear, the meat is cooked.

Variation
Use blackberries instead of blackcurrants in this recipe.

Serving Idea
Serve with a selection of fresh green vegetables.

SERVES 4
220 kilocalories per serving

KIDNEYS WITH MUSTARD SAUCE

Lambs' kidneys have a wonderful delicate flavor, and when served with a delicious mustard sauce, make a quick and very flavorful main course.

5 tbsps vegetable oil
1½lbs lambs' kidneys
1-2 shallots, peeled and finely chopped
1⅓ cups dry white wine
3¾ tbsps Dijon mustard
Salt, pepper and lemon juice to taste
2½ tbsps fresh chopped parsley

1. Cut the kidneys in half lengthwise, and carefully snip out the core and tough tubes.

2. Heat the oil in a large frying pan, and gently sauté the kidneys for about 10 minutes, stirring them frequently until they are light brown on all sides. Remove the kidneys from the pan and keep them warm.

3. Add the shallots to the sauté pan and cook for about 1 minute, stirring frequently until they soften, but do not brown.

4. Add the wine and bring to the boil, stirring constantly and scraping the pan to remove any brown juices.

5. Allow the wine to boil rapidly for 3-4 minutes, until it has reduced by about 2/3rds. Remove the pan from the heat.

6. Using an eggbeater or fork, mix the mustard into the reduced wine along with salt, pepper, lemon juice to taste, and half of the fresh chopped parsley.

7. Return the kidneys to the pan and cook over a low heat for 1-2 minutes, stirring all the time to heat the kidneys through evenly. Serve immediately, sprinkled with the remaining parsley.

Step 1 Trim any fat or tubes away from the core of each kidney, using a sharp knife or small pair of scissors.

Step 2 Sauté the kidneys in the hot oil, stirring them frequently to brown evenly on all sides.

Step 6 Using an eggbeater or fork, blend the mustard into the reduced wine, whisking well to keep the sauce smooth.

Cook's Notes

Time
Preparation takes about 25 minutes, cooking takes 15 minutes.

Variation
Use chicken livers in place of the lambs' kidney in this recipe.

Watchpoint
Take care not to cook the kidneys for too long as they will toughen if overcooked.

SERVES 4

254 kilocalories per serving

SOLE KEBABS

Fish is highly nutritious, economical to prepare, and makes an ideal contribution to a healthy diet.

8 fillets of sole
5 tbsps olive oil
1 clove garlic, minced
Juice ½ lemon
Finely grated rind ½ lemon
Salt and freshly ground black pepper
3 drops of Tabasco, or pepper sauce
3 medium-sized zucchini
1 medium-sized green pepper
Freshly chopped parsley for garnish

1. Using a sharp knife, carefully peel the skin from the backs of each sole fillet.

Step 1 Use a sharp knife to carefully cut between the meat of the fish and the skin. Lift the meat up and away as you cut, keeping the blade of the knife away from you.

Step 2 Cut the sole fillets in half lengthwise, and roll the slices up jelly roll fashion.

2. Cut each sole fillet in half lengthwise, and roll each slice up jelly roll fashion.

3. Mix together the oil, garlic, lemon juice, rind, and seasonings in a small bowl.

4. Put the rolls of fish into a shallow dish and pour over the lemon and oil marinade. Cover the dish and allow to stand in a cool place for at least 2 hours.

5. Cut the zucchini into ¼-inch slices.

6. Cut the peppers in half lengthwise and remove the white core and the seeds. Chop the pepper flesh into 1-inch squares.

7. Carefully thread the marinated sole fillets onto kebab skewers, alternating these with pieces of the prepared vegetables. Brush each kebab with a little of the oil and lemon marinade.

8. Arrange the kebabs on a broiler pan and cook under a moderately hot broiler for about 8 minutes, turning frequently to prevent them from burning, and brushing with the extra marinade to keep them moist.

9. Arrange the kebabs on a serving dish, and sprinkle with the chopped parsley for garnish.

Step 7 Thread the marinated rolls of fish onto kebab skewers, alternating these with vegetables for color.

Cook's Notes

Time
Preparation takes about 30 minutes, plus marinating time. Cooking takes approximately 8 minutes.

Preparation
After 2 hours marinating, the sole will look opaque and have a partially cooked appearance.

Cook's Tip
These kebabs are ideal for cooking out of doors on a barbeque.

SERVES 6
275 kilocalories per serving

CASSEROLE OF VEAL AND MUSHROOMS

Veal is a low fat meat and is delicious when served in this tomato and mushroom sauce.

3lbs lean pie veal
Salt and freshly ground black pepper
5 tbsps olive oil
2 shallots, finely chopped
½ clove garlic, minced
½ cup dry white wine
1⅓ cups strong brown stock
1 cup canned tomatoes, drained and chopped
1 bouquet garni
2 strips lemon peel
1 cup small button mushrooms
2½ tbsps fresh chopped parsley

1. Dice the meat into bite-sized pieces, using a sharp knife.

2. Sprinkle the pieces of meat with salt and pepper, then allow to stand for about 30 minutes.

3. Heat half of the oil in a large frying pan, and cook the pieces of meat for 5-10 minutes, stirring them frequently until they are browned on all sides. Remove the meat from the pan and set it aside.

4. Add the shallots and garlic to the oil and meat juices in the pan, lower the heat and cook until softened, but not colored. Return the veal to the pan and mix well.

5. Add the wine, stock, tomatoes, bouquet garni and lemon peel to the meat mixture, and bring to the boil.

6. Transfer the veal to an ovenproof casserole. Cover with a tight-fitting lid and bake in a pre-heated oven 325°F for

Step 3 Gently brown the veal in the hot oil, stirring it frequently until it has browned on all sides.

Step 4 Cook the garlic and shallots in the hot oil and meat juices gently, taking care to soften, but not brown them.

about 1¼ hours, or until the meat is tender.

7. Heat the remaining oil in a clean frying pan, and gently stir in the mushrooms, cooking them for 2-3 minutes until they begin to soften, but are not properly cooked.

8. After the casserole cooking time has finished, stir in the partially cooked mushrooms and continue cooking in the oven for a further 15 minutes.

9. Sprinkle with the chopped parsley before serving.

Cook's Notes

Time
Preparation takes about 30 minutes, cooking takes approximately 1½ hours.

Variation
Use lamb, or beef, instead of the veal in this recipe.

Serving Idea
Serve with new potatoes, pasta, or rice.

Watchpoint
Do not allow the garlic and onions to brown, or it will impair the flavor of the veal.

SERVES 4
157 kilocalories per serving

EGGPLANT AND CHICKEN CHILI

This unusual dish is both delicious and filling.

2 medium-sized eggplants
5 tbsps sesame oil
2 cloves garlic, minced
4 green onions
1 green chili, finely chopped
¾lb boned and skinned chicken breast
5 tbsps light soy sauce
2½ tbsps stock, or water
1¼ tbsps tomato paste
1 tsp cornstarch
Liquid sweetener to taste

Step 6 Cut the green onions diagonally into small pieces, approximately ½ inch long.

1. Cut the eggplant into quarters lengthwise, using a sharp knife. Slice the eggplant quarters into pieces approximately ½-inch thick.

2. Put the eggplant slices into a bowl and sprinkle liberally with salt. Stir well to coat evenly. Cover with plastic wrap and leave to stand for 30 minutes.

3. Rinse the eggplant slices very thoroughly under running water, then pat dry with a clean tea cloth.

4. Heat half of the oil in a wok, or large frying pan, and gently cook the garlic until it is soft, but not colored.

5. Add the eggplant slices to the wok and cook, stirring frequently, for 3-4 minutes.

6. Using a sharp knife, slice the green onions into thin diagonal strips. Stir the green onions together with the chili into the cooked eggplant, and cook for a further 1 minute. Remove the eggplant and onion from the pan, and set aside, keeping warm.

7. Cut the chicken breast into thin slices with a sharp knife.

8. Heat the remaining oil in the wok, and fry the chicken pieces for approximately 2 minutes or until they have turned white and are cooked thoroughly.

9. Return the eggplant and onions to the pan and cook, stirring continuously, for 2 minutes or until heated through completely.

10. Mix together the remaining ingredients and pour these over the chicken and eggplants in the wok, stirring constantly until the sauce has thickened and cleared. Serve immediately.

Cook's Notes

Time
Preparation takes about 10 minutes, cooking takes approximately 15 minutes.

Cook's Tip
The vegetables can be prepared well in advance, but the eggplants should be removed from the salt after 30 minutes, or they will become too dehydrated.

Variation
Use turkey instead of chicken in this recipe, and zucchini in place of the eggplants.

Serving Idea
Serve this recipe as part of a more extensive Chinese style meal.

SERVES 4
170 kilocalories per serving
FRUIT PLATE

This medley of fruit can be varied to suit your taste and is served without a syrupy liquid, so is low in calories.

1 green fig
2 kiwi fruit
2 fresh dates
1 guava
1 paw paw
¾ cup lychees
½ small pineapple
1 fresh mango
¾ cup seedless grapes
½ small melon
½lb watermelon
2½ tbsps orange juice
2½ tbsps lemon juice
½ cup chopped walnuts, or pine kernels (optional)

1. Select a large, shallow serving platter on which to arrange the fruit.

2. Cut the figs into quarters lengthwise and arrange on a plate.

3. Peel the kiwi fruits, and remove any hard core from the stem end. Slice the fruit thinly and arrange alongside the figs, reserving a few slices for the watermelon.

4. Cut the dates in half lengthwise and remove the stones. Place the dates on the serving plate.

5. Cut the guavas in half and slice these into wedges with a sharp knife. Peel the paw paw and slice this into thin crescents. Arrange the guava slices and paw paw alternately onto the plate along with the other prepared fruit.

6. Peel the lychees and remove the stones from the stalk end, using the rounded tip of a swivel potato peeler. Discard the stones, and place the fruit on the serving platter.

7. Peel the pineapple and cut away any brown eyes which may remain in the flesh. Cut the pineapple into slices and remove the core, using a sharp knife or apple corer. Cut the pineapple slices into small wedges and arrange on the plate.

8. Peel the mango and cut the flesh into slices, discarding the stone.

9. Halve the seedless grapes. Place the mango and grapes in an alternate pattern, alongside the rest of the fruit on the serving plate.

10. Peel the melon, cut into half, and remove the seeds. Slice the melon flesh into small wedges.

11. Leave the peel and pips in the watermelon, and cut this into small wedges, approximately the same size as the previous melon. Arrange the melon wedges on either side of the plate and decorate with the remaining kiwi fruit if used.

12. Mix together the lemon, juice, orange juice and chopped nuts, and sprinkle this dressing evenly over the fruit on the plate. Cover with plastic wrap and chill well before serving.

Step 6 Remove the stones from the lychees by scooping them out from the stalk end with the rounded end of a potato peeler.

Cook's Notes

Time
Preparation takes about 30 minutes, plus chiling time.

Preparation
Canned lychees could be used in place of the fresh fruit in this recipe, as could canned pineapples, kiwis and mangoes, but make sure they are packed in natural juice which should be drained before serving.

Variation
Use any selection of your favorite fruits in this recipe.

SERVES 4
63 kilocalories per serving
STRAWBERRY YOGURT ICE

Ice cream is usually forbidden on a low calorie diet, but when prepared with low fat natural yogurt and fresh fruit, it can provide a welcome treat.

1⅔ cups fresh strawberries
1⅓ cups low fat natural yogurt
2½ tsps gelatin
2½ tbsps boiling water
1 egg white
Liquid sweetener to taste
Few fresh strawberries for decoration

1. Remove and discard the green stalks and leaves from the top of the strawberries. Roughly chop the fruit.

2. Place the strawberries into a liquidizer, or food processor, along with the yogurt. Blend until smooth.

3. Sprinkle the gelatin over the boiling water in a small bowl. Stand the bowl into another, and pour in enough boiling water to come halfway up the sides of the dish.

4. Allow the gelatin to stand, without stirring, until it has dissolved and the liquid has cleared.

5. Pour the strawberry mixture into a bowl, and stir in the dissolved gelatin, mixing well to blend evenly. Place the bowl into a deep freeze and chill until just icy around the edges.

6. Remove the bowl from the deep freeze and beat until the chilled mixture is smooth. Return the bowl to the deep freeze and freeze once again in the same way.

7. Remove the bowl from the deep freeze a second time, and whisk with an electric mixer until smooth. Whisk the egg white until it forms soft peaks.

8. Fold the whisked egg white into the partially set straw-

Step 2 Blend the strawberries and yogurt together in a liquidizer or food processor, until they are smooth.

Step 5 Remove the strawberry mixture from the freezer when it is just beginning to set and has frozen around the edges.

berry mixture, carefully lifting and cutting the mixture to keep it light.

9. Sweeten with liquid sweetener to taste, then pour the strawberry ice into a shallow sided ice cream dish, and return to the freezer to freeze until completely set.

10. Remove the ice cream 10 minutes before serving to soften slightly. Pile into serving dishes and decorate with a few extra strawberries.

Cook's Notes

Time
Preparation takes about 15 minutes, plus freezing time.

Cook's Tip
Use frozen or canned strawberries in place of the fresh strawberries, but drain all the juice away first.

Variation
Use any other soft fruit in place of the strawberries. It may be preferable to sieve blackcurrants or raspberries to remove the pips, before adding to the yogurt as a purée.

SERVES 4
109 kilocalories per serving

BLACKBERRY FLUFF

Fresh blackberries have a delicious flavor, especially the wild ones picked from hedgerows.

1lb fresh blackberries
1⅓ cups natural low fat set yogurt
2 egg whites
Liquid sweetener to taste
Pieces of angelica and whole blackberries to decorate

---

1. Wash the blackberries thoroughly and place them in a saucepan with no extra water, other than that which is left on their surfaces after washing. Cover the pan with a tight fitting lid, and cook over a low heat for 5-10 minutes, stirring occasionally until the fruit has softened. Cool slightly.

2. Press the cooked blackberries through a nylon sieve, using the back of a spoon to press out the juice and pulp. Discard the pips and reserve the purée.

3. Put the yogurt into a large bowl and beat in the blackberry purée until it is smooth.

4. Whisk the egg whites until they form very stiff peaks.

5. Fold these into the blackberry purée, trying not to over mix the ingredients, so as to create an attractive marbled effect.

6. Sweeten with the liquid sweetener to taste, then pile into serving dishes and decorate with the whole blackberries and angelica pieces. Chill before serving.

Step 4 Whisk the egg whites until they form very stiff peaks.

Step 2 Press the cooked blackberries through a metal sieve, using the back of a wooden spoon to push through the juice and pulp, leaving the pips in the sieve.

Step 5 Lightly fold the egg whites into the blackberry mixture, to create an attractive marbled effect.

Cook's Notes

Time
Preparation takes about 20 minutes. Cooking time takes approximately 10 minutes, plus chilling time.

Preparation
This recipe can also be partially frozen to create a cooling summer dessert.

Variation
Use raspberries, or strawberries, in place of blackberries in this recipe.

SERVES 4
101 kilocalories per serving

SUNBURST FIGS

Fresh figs can make a most attractive dessert and have the added benefit of being very low in calories.

4 fresh figs
⅔ cup redcurrants in small bunches
6 oranges
1¼ tsps orange flower water

1. Trim the stalks away from the top of the figs, but do not peel them.

2. Cut the figs into quarters lengthwise, taking care not to sever them completely at the base.

Step 2 Cut the figs into quarters lengthwise with a sharp knife, taking great care not to sever the fruit completely through the base.

3. Press the fig quarters open gently with your fingers, to make a flower shape. Place each fig carefully on a serving plate.

4. Arrange the small bunches of redcurrants carefully on the center of each fig.

5. Cut 2 of the oranges in half, and squeeze out the juice. Mix this juice with the orange flower water in a small jug.

6. Carefully cut away the peel and white pith from the re-

Step 3 Carefully press open the quarters of each fig to make an attractive flower shape.

Step 7 Cut the orange segments away from the peeled fruit with a sharp knife, slicing carefully between the flesh and the thin membranes inside each segment.

maining 4 oranges.

7. Using a sharp knife, cut the segments of orange away from the inside of the thin membranes, keeping each piece intact as a crescent shape.

8. Arrange the orange segments in between the petals of the fig flower on the serving plate.

9. Spoon equal amounts of the orange sauce over each fig, and chill thoroughly before serving.

Cook's Notes

Time
Preparation takes about 15 minutes, plus chiling time.

Variation
Use ruby grapefruit segments and blackcurrants in place of the oranges and redcurrants in this recipe.

Serving Idea
Freeze the currants before placing them on the figs, to give an attractive finish to this dessert.

SERVES 4
125 kilocalories per serving

MANGO SORBET

This delicious cool sorbet can be used either as a dessert, or as a refresher between courses on a low calorie meal.

3 mangoes
Juice ½ lime
½ cup dry white wine
½ cup mineral water
1 egg white
Liquid sweetener to taste (optional)

1. Peel the mango and cut away the flesh from around the large center stone.

2. Put the mango flesh into a liquidizer or food processor, and blend until smooth.

3. In a bowl, mix together the lime juice, wine and mineral water.

4. Place the mango purée in a freezer and freeze until just beginning to set around the edges.

5. Break up the ice crystals in the mango mixture using a fork.

6. Whisk the egg white until it is stiff, then fold this carefully and thoroughly into the mango mixture. Sweeten with liquid sweetener to taste, if used.

7. Return the mango mixture to the deep freeze, and freeze until completely set.

8. To serve, remove from the deep freeze 10 minutes before required, then spoon into individual serving dishes.

Step 2 Purée the mango flesh in a liquidizer or food processor, until it is smooth.

Step 5 Break up the ice crystals which have formed in the mango mixture into small pieces using the back of a fork.

Cook's Notes

Time
Preparation takes about 15 minutes, plus freezing time.

Variation
Use any other favorite fruit in place of the mango.

Serving Idea
Serve with fresh fruit.

INDEX